The Don't Laugh Challenge™

7 YEAR OLD EDITION

Don't Laugh Challenge
BONUS PLAY

Join our Joke Club and get the Bonus Play PDF!

Simply send us an email to:

 bacchuspublish@gmail.com

and you will get the following:

• 10 BONUS hilarious jokes!

• An entry in our Monthly Giveaway of a
$25 Amazon Gift card!

We draw a new winner each month and will contact you via email!

Good luck!

Welcome to
The Don't Laugh Challenge ™

• How do you play?

The Don't Laugh Challenge is made up of 10 rounds with 2 games in each round. It is a 2-3 player game with the players being 'Jester #1','Jester #2', and a 'King' or 'Queen'. In each game you have an opportunity to score points by making the other players laugh.

After completing each round, tally up the points to determine the Round Champion! Add all 10 rounds together to see who is the Ultimate Don't Laugh Challenge Master! If you end up in a tie, use our final Tie Breaker Round for a Winner Takes All!

• Who can play the game?

Get the whole family involved! Grab a family member or a friend and take turns going back and forth. We've also added Bonus Points in game 2, so grab a 3rd person, a.k.a 'King' or 'Queen', and earn an extra point by making them guess your scene!

The Don't Laugh Challenge™
Activity Rules

- ## Game 1 - Jokes (1 point each)

  Jester #1 will hold the book and read each joke to
  Jester #2. If the joke makes Jester #2 laugh, Jester #1
  can record a point for the joke. Each joke is worth 1
  point. At the end of the jokes, tally up your total Joke
  Points scored for Jester #1 and continue to Game 2!

- ## Game 2 - Silly Scenarios
  ## (2 points each + bonus point)

  Without telling the other Jester what the scenarios say,
  read each scenario to yourself and then get creative by
  acting it out! You can use sound effects, but be sure not
  to say any words! If you make the other Jester laugh,
  record your points and continue to the next scenario.

  BONUS POINT: Get your parents or a third player, a.k.a
  King or Queen, involved and have them guess what in the
  world you are doing! Get the King or Queen to guess
  the scene correctly and you score a BONUS POINT!

The Don't Laugh Challenge ™
Activity Rules

Once Jester #1 completes both games it is Jester #2's turn. The directions at the bottom of the book will tell you who goes next. Once you have both completed all the games in the round, add your total points from each game to the Round Score Page and record the Round winner!

- ## How do you get started?

Flip a coin. If guessed correctly, then that Jester begins!

Tip: Make any of the activities extra funny by using facial expressions, funny voices or silly movements!

Jokes

Knock knock.
Who's there?
Handsome.   /1
Handsome, who?
Handsome money over!

What did the label say to the
jar?   /1

"I'm totally stuck on you."

What do you call a clumsy
insect?   /1

A Stumble Bee!

What do you call it when a   /1
snail travels back to the past?

'Slime travel'.

JOKES TOTAL: _____ /4

Silly Scenarios

(Act it out!)

You're a cat prowling the streets when suddenly it starts to rain... and you HATE water! Be vocal with your meows as you search for cover!

_____ /2

You're a fish that has just been caught by a fisherman! Get on the floor and pretend to flop and gasp for air like a fish out of water!

_____ /2

SILLY SCENARIOS TOTAL: _____ /4

NOW, PASS THE BOOK TO JESTER 2 ➝

Jokes

Why did the nervous polar bear jump?

He was trying to break the ice!   /1

What dog do you take on a dinner date?

A Dalmatian. They always know what
hits the SPOT!   /1

What do cobras order at Dairy Queen?

Milk-SNAKES!   /1

What has dozens of keys, but none of them unlock anything?

/1

A computer!

JOKES TOTAL: _____ /4

Silly Scenarios

(Act it out!)

You are the roughest, toughest and rowdiest cowboy in town! Unfortunately, you are terrible at riding horses. Keep falling off!

_____ /2

Pretend you are a new baby chick, chirping and fighting to break out of your shell! Show everyone what it's like to see the world for the first time!

_____ /2

SILLY SCENARIOS TOTAL: _____ /4

TIME TO SCORE YOUR POINTS! ➡

JESTER 1

/8

ROUND TOTAL

JESTER 2

/8

ROUND TOTAL

ROUND
CHAMPION

ROUND
2

Jokes

Why does dinosaur insurance cost so much?

Because of all the t-wrecks!

/1

Did you hear about the famous cow?

He was Legen-DAIRY!

/1

What do you call an invisible spider?

Absolutely terrifying.

/1

What do you call a dog with magical powers?

The Wizard of Paws.

/1

JOKES TOTAL: _____ /4

  JESTER 1 CONTINUE TO THE NEXT PAGE ➡

Silly Scenarios

(Act it out!)

Pretend you're an old man/woman looking for a seat to sit down. You squint to see and use your cane to walk while looking around, then sit on your friend, thinking they are a chair!

/2

You are a penguin waddling on slippery ice and you can't seem to find your balance. Do anything you can to keep from falling!

/2

SILLY SCENARIOS TOTAL: /4

NOW, PASS THE BOOK TO JESTER 2 ➡

Jokes

What kind of business does Eeyore like to work in?

Re-TAIL.

/1

What do you call something that can measure everything?

The Ruler of All.

/1

Why are flies annoying?

They always BUG people!

/1

Where do skunks like to go on Spring Break?

SPRAY-cation!

/1

JOKES TOTAL: _____ /4

JESTER 2 CONTINUE TO THE NEXT PAGE →

Silly Scenarios

(Act it out!)

Imagine you are a ceiling fan. You have 3 speeds... Low, Medium, and High. Show how you go through all the speeds, until suddenly, you come to an immediate STOP!

/2

Someone put glue in your hat and it's really stuck! Keep trying to take it off and once you finally do, pretend to fall back to the ground and act exhausted!

/2

SILLY SCENARIOS TOTAL: _____ /4

TIME TO SCORE YOUR POINTS! ➜

JESTER 1

/8
___
ROUND TOTAL

JESTER 2

/8
___
ROUND TOTAL

___

ROUND CHAMPION

ROUND 3

Jokes

How do you make a King laugh?

Turn his crown upside down!

/1

What did the lamp say to the blown-out candle?

"Hey, man! Lighten up!"

/1

What did the squirrel tell the dog, when he got the wrong address?

"You're barking up the wrong tree!"

/1

Why shouldn't you play cards with mountains?

They PEAK!

/1

JOKES TOTAL: _____ /4

24

JESTER 1 CONTINUE TO THE NEXT PAGE ➡

Silly Scenarios

(Act it out!)

You are a true one-man band. Rock out on every instrument! (Tip: Use your body as a drum and sounds for the full effect!)

_____ /2

It's dinner time and no matter how hard you try, you can't get the last bit of ketchup out of the bottle. Get creative, anything to get that last drop!!

_____ /2

SILLY SCENARIOS TOTAL: _____ /4

NOW, PASS THE BOOK TO JESTER 2 ➡

Jokes

What do you call a bear with no teeth?

A Gummy Bear.

/1

What is Mario's favorite pie on Thanksgiving?

A pizza pie!

/1

What do trains say to express their love?

"I choo-choose you!"

/1

Where does a baseball player put his food?

On home plate.

/1

JOKES TOTAL: _____ /4

JESTER 2 CONTINUE TO THE NEXT PAGE ➡

Silly Scenarios

(Act it out!)

While eating popcorn, you toss a kernel in the air and catch it in your mouth! How fun! Spin, dive, and move around the room with energy while you keep throwing and catching more pieces in your mouth!

/2

You're a frog who likes to do karate. Do a few frog leaps, before you hop up and do a giant KARATE CHOP! (Tip: Use sound effects!)

/2

SILLY SCENARIOS TOTAL: _____ /4

TIME TO SCORE YOUR POINTS! ➡

JESTER 1

/8
ROUND TOTAL

JESTER 2

/8
ROUND TOTAL

ROUND CHAMPION

ROUND 4

Jokes

What does a hammer say when it does something well?

"Nailed it!"

/1

What did the owl say to the other owl, when they left the party?

"Well, that was a hoot!"

/1

What kind of insect can hold up an entire house?

A Cater-PILLAR.

/1

How was the fish forgiven?

He was let off the hook.

/1

JOKES TOTAL: _____ /4

30

JESTER 1 CONTINUE TO THE NEXT PAGE ➡

Silly Scenarios

(Act it out!)

You are a T-Rex with short arms and you are trying to tie your shoe. Let out a big dinosaur sigh when you **FINALLY** get it!

/2

While eating a delicious, extremely cheesy pizza slice, you struggle to swallow because the cheese is never-ending! Make your eyes huge and keep trying to finish that bite!

/2

SILLY SCENARIOS TOTAL: _____ /4

NOW, PASS THE BOOK TO JESTER 2 ➜

Jokes

What do you call a heart who eats too much sugar?

Sweetheart!

/1

What do you call a good looking grill?

Barbe-CUTE!

/1

**Knock knock.
Who's there?
He.
He, who?
Oh, I didn't know you could speak Donkey!**

/1

What underwater creature would be good for the Circus?

/1

A Clownfish!

JOKES TOTAL: _____ /4

Silly Scenarios

(Act it out!)

OH NO! An office building is on fire and you're the first firefighter on at the scene! Grab the water hose and show how you put out those giant flames with confidence!

/2

You are VERY sleepy and can barely keep your eyes open. Keep trying to stay awake by pretending to slap yourself, holding your eyes open, or even shaking your head... but still, you fall asleep!

/2

SILLY SCENARIOS TOTAL: _____ /4

TIME TO SCORE YOUR POINTS! ➜

JESTER 1

/8

ROUND TOTAL

JESTER 2

/8

ROUND TOTAL

ROUND CHAMPION

ROUND
5

Jokes

What's brown, gooey, and sometimes a little runny?

Peanut Butter!

/1

What kind of keys can't open doors?

Mon-KEYS!

/1

Why didn't the snail feel like getting out of bed?

He was feeling quite sluggish.

/1

Why are ideas so cheap?

Well, it's only a penny for your thoughts!

/1

JOKES TOTAL: _____ /4

Silly Scenarios

(Act it out!)

While taking your clothes out of the dryer to fold, they are way too HOT! Keep trying while tossing them up like a hot potato!

/2

It's time for your evening walk, and your feet suddenly weigh 50 lbs. each. You can drag them, slide them or use your hands, but you can't seem to lift them off the ground!

/2

SILLY SCENARIOS TOTAL: _____ /4

NOW, PASS THE BOOK TO JESTER 2 ➡

Jokes

What do cows like to do on the weekend?

Go to the **MOO**-vies!

/1

What is the best road for seeds?

Sesame Street!

/1

What do you call a sleeping Stegosaurus?

A Dino-SNORE!

/1

What do ghosts tie their shoes with?

Boo-laces!

/1

JOKES TOTAL: _____ /4

 JESTER 2 CONTINUE TO THE NEXT PAGE ➔

Silly Scenarios

(Act it out!)

Elephants can never pass up a good watering hole. Use your trunk to spray yourself clean for the day and show how much you LOVE the water!

/2

You decided to go on a walk and accidentally stepped in dog poop. It smells very, VERY bad! Make a gross face and pretend to try to wipe it off on your friends!

/2

SILLY SCENARIOS TOTAL: _____ /4

TIME TO SCORE YOUR POINTS! ➔

JESTER 1

/8

ROUND TOTAL

JESTER 2

/8

ROUND TOTAL

ROUND CHAMPION

ROUND

6

Jokes

What do you tell a dog that won't sit still?

Paws! (Pause)

/1

Why do people think the ocean is sad?

It's always blue!

/1

How do crocodiles stay hydrated?

They drink a lot of GATOR-ade!

/1

What do you call it when a dog swallows a wedding ring?

A diamond in the RUFF!

/1

JOKES TOTAL: ____ /4

JESTER 1 CONTINUE TO THE NEXT PAGE ➡

Silly Scenarios

(Act it out!)

You're a hungry woodpecker, working on making a hole in a tree to get some food. As you're pecking on the tree, you get a giant worm! SCORE! Gobble it up, happily!

/2

You're a curious beetle exploring your environment. Uh-oh! You got flipped upside down on your back and can't seem to get back up! Keep trying!

/2

SILLY SCENARIOS TOTAL: _____ /4

 NOW, PASS THE BOOK TO JESTER 2 ➤

Jokes

Why is the ice cube so popular?

He's the coolest.

/1

What is the alphabet's favorite kind of food?

C-food! (Seafood)

/1

Why can a cat always cheer you up?

They are so paws-itive!

/1

Where do plants go when they're sleepy?

To the garden bed!

/1

JOKES TOTAL: _____ /4

JESTER 2 CONTINUE TO THE NEXT PAGE ➡

Silly Scenarios

(Act it out!)

You are a champion jumping frog. In your third jump, an irresistible swarm of delicious bugs flies across your path. Go crazy chasing and eating them!

_____ /2

You need to sneeze but can't find a tissue. When you finally sneeze into your hands, you blow out a sticky wad of boogers and now you don't know where to wipe it. GROSS!!

_____ /2

SILLY SCENARIOS TOTAL: _____ /4

TIME TO SCORE YOUR POINTS! ➡

JESTER 1

/8

ROUND TOTAL

JESTER 2

/8

ROUND TOTAL

ROUND CHAMPION

ROUND

7

Jokes

Why do chickens have bad tempers?

Their buddies are always egging them on! _____ /1

Why do gorillas have such big nostrils?

Because they have big fingers! _____ /1

Knock knock.
Who's there?
Poor me.
Poor me, who?
Poor me some lemonade! I'm thirsty!

_____ /1

Did the grizzly pass his math test?

_____ /1

BEAR-ly!

JOKES TOTAL: _____ /4

Silly Scenarios

(Act it out!)

Pretend time suddenly slowed down and you have to walk in slow motion. Act really confused while looking around and moving slowly, but be careful not to fall!

_____ /2

While eating a sandwich you notice your mouth is on FIRE! You look down surprised and see that someone put spicy peppers in it. Show how spicy it is!

_____ /2

SILLY SCENARIOS TOTAL: _____ /4

 NOW, PASS THE BOOK TO JESTER 2 ➡

Jokes

What is one bow you can never tie?

A rainbow!

/1

How did the alien turn the human into a couch potato?

They used a LAZY-er beam!

/1

How do you send a package to Mars?

/1

You space-ship it!

Where do army fish live?

In tanks!

/1

JOKES TOTAL: _____ /4

Silly Scenarios

(Act it out!)

You are enjoying an ice cream cone, but the ice cream falls off on the first lick. You still want to eat it, so do you scoop it back into your cone or eat it off the floor? Show the crowd!

/2

While walking through a big forest and admiring all the trees, you notice that there are spider webs EVERYWHERE! Fling your arms, move quickly, and run to get away! AHH!

/2

SILLY SCENARIOS TOTAL: /4

TIME TO SCORE YOUR POINTS! ➡

JESTER 1

/8

ROUND TOTAL

JESTER 2

/8

ROUND TOTAL

ROUND CHAMPION

ROUND

8

Jokes

What did the monkey say to the sloth during a high-five?

"Too slow!" ____ /1

Why did the rooster get off the rollercoaster?

He chickened out! ____ /1

I didn't understand why the pen took off it's cap, but now I see it's point!

____ /1

What do you call a flattered cat?

A Smitten Kitten! ____ /1

JOKES TOTAL: ____ /4

54

Silly Scenarios

(Act it out!) JESTER 1

You are a cat wanting attention from your friend, the owner. Demonstrate how you would get your owners attention and show them what you want by meowing, hissing, rubbing on their legs, etc.

_____ /2

You are a little elf playing the flute as you dance and skip around. Don't forget to add some elf dance moves!

_____ /2

SILLY SCENARIOS TOTAL: _____ /4

NOW, PASS THE BOOK TO JESTER 2 →

Jokes

What do you call a flock of lambs sleeping in the living room?

/1

A SHEEP-over!

Why did the bike stop?

He was TIRE-D.

/1

What kind of soda do you find at hospitals?

Dr. Pepper

/1

Do elephants use suitcases?

No, they prefer to use a trunk.

/1

JOKES TOTAL: ____ /4

JESTER 2 CONTINUE TO THE NEXT PAGE ➜

Silly Scenarios

(Act it out!)

You have been sitting all day in your boat, trying to fish. You haven't caught anything yet, but suddenly you feel a pull on your line and it's a BIG one! Do your best to reel it in!

_____ /2

Pretend to be a cute kitten trying to get adopted at the shelter. Be extra cute by purring, pawing through your cage, and giving your best, big kitten eyes!

_____ /2

SILLY SCENARIOS TOTAL: _____ /4

TIME TO SCORE YOUR POINTS! ➡

JESTER 1

/8

ROUND TOTAL

JESTER 2

/8

ROUND TOTAL

ROUND CHAMPION

ROUND 9

Jokes

How did the Queen Bee tell her child to calm down?

"Honeybee quiet!"

/1

What do you call a horse that lives next to you?

A neeeigghh-bor.

/1

What is a monkey's favorite number?

Tree!

/1

What do you get when you cross a lizard, a dog, and a pirate?

/1

A Scally Wag!

JOKES TOTAL: _____ /4

JESTER 1 CONTINUE TO THE NEXT PAGE

Silly Scenarios

(Act it out!)

Do your very best "flossing" dance move while acting like a giant gorilla! Don't forget to end with a big gorilla chest pound!

_____ /2

You are Frankenstein being woken up for the first time. Try out the new body by moving around, but it's super stiff and needs to be broken in!

_____ /2

SILLY SCENARIOS TOTAL: _____ /4

 STOP

NOW, PASS THE BOOK TO JESTER 2 ➔

Jokes

What do you call a soccer tournament for dogs?

'The World Pup!'

/1

What has eight legs and would make a great secret agent?

A SPY-der.

/1

Where is the superhero 'Slothman' from?

Slothem City.

/1

Why did the teddy bear skip brunch?

It was already stuffed!

/1

JOKES TOTAL: _____ /4

Silly Scenarios

(Act it out!)

You're a penguin and a polar bear is chasing you! QUICK! Waddle behind an iceberg and hide, but make sure to check if it's safe to come out before you waddle back.

/2

You are a fearsome lion, King of the ferocious beasts! You have a great big roar, and you love to sing with it! Show the other lions how it's done!

/2

SILLY SCENARIOS TOTAL: _____ /4

TIME TO SCORE YOUR POINTS! ➡

JESTER 1

/8

ROUND TOTAL

JESTER 2

/8

ROUND TOTAL

ROUND CHAMPION

ROUND 10

Jokes

What do you call a talented fish?

A Star-fish!

_____ /1

What's little, red and black, and curtsies?

A Ladybug!

_____ /1

What did the Investigator say, when he walked by the seafood market?

"Something smells fishy here..."

_____ /1

What card game is Ariel's favorite?

Go Fish!

_____ /1

JOKES TOTAL: _____ /4

JESTER 1 CONTINUE TO THE NEXT PAGE ➔

Silly Scenarios

(Act it out!)

Act like a sneaky snake slithering on the floor (don't use your arms!) to get to the ice cream. Show what a snake eating ice cream looks like and end with a satisfying hiss!

_____ /2

You're a waiter/waitress carrying a big tray of food and drinks to a table - **OOPS!** You step on a slippery spot on the floor and try your best to get back your balance! Don't drop the tray!

_____ /2

SILLY SCENARIOS TOTAL: _____ /4

NOW, PASS THE BOOK TO JESTER 2 ➜

Jokes

Why are spiders so smart?

They're really good at using the web!

/1

What is the frog's favorite music?

Hip-HOP!

/1

What do cats say when they get all the questions right on a test?

"Purrrrrfect!"

/1

Why did the alien leave his planet?

It needed some SPACE!

/1

JOKES TOTAL: _____ /4

JESTER 2 CONTINUE TO THE NEXT PAGE ➡

Silly Scenarios

(Act it out!)

You're on stage accepting the award for "World's Longest Tongue", but every time you open your mouth to try and give your speech, your giant tongue falls out! This ends up making you mumble your acceptance speech!

_____ /2

Pretend you have a hula hoop on! Wiggle your hips and see how long you can go without dropping it!

_____ /2

SILLY SCENARIOS TOTAL: _____ /4

TIME TO SCORE YOUR POINTS! ➡

JESTER 1

/8

ROUND TOTAL

JESTER 2

/8

ROUND TOTAL

ROUND CHAMPION

ADD UP ALL YOUR POINTS FROM EACH ROUND.
THE PLAYER WITH THE MOST POINTS IS CROWNED
THE ULTIMATE LAUGH MASTER!

IN THE EVENT OF A TIE, CONTINUE TO THE ROUND
11 FOR THE TIE-BREAKER ROUND!

 **JESTER 1** _____

GRAND TOTAL

 **JESTER 2** _____

GRAND TOTAL

_____

**THE ULTIMATE
DON'T LAUGH CHALLENGE MASTER**

ROUND
11
TIE-BREAKER
(WINNER TAKES ALL!)

Jokes

What does a gopher do when a coyote comes to town?

Go-pher help!

/1

**Knock knock.
Who's there?
Tish.
Tish, who?
No thanks, I've got a napkin right here.**

/1

Peter Pan's beloved fairy friend reeked of a stench from not showering. What was her name?

STINKER Bell!

/1

What do you call a dog who isn't potty trained?

/1

Puddles.

JOKES TOTAL: _____ /4

JESTER 1 CONTINUE TO THE NEXT PAGE ➡

Silly Scenarios

(Act it out!)

You are a silly monkey! Walk on all fours, eat bananas, or shake your butt! Just make sure to show off your best monkey impression and noises!

/2

You're one of the strongest humans in the world and working on setting the world record for lifting, but suddenly, you feel a rumble in your tummy. Oh no... every lift makes you pass gas! (Use silly fart noises!)

/2

SILLY SCENARIOS TOTAL: _____ /4

 NOW, PASS THE BOOK TO JESTER 2 ➡

Jokes

Why do you call a ticklish tent?

A happy camper!

_____ /1

Which state is the cleanest in the United States?

WASH-ington, of course!

_____ /1

What are bears least favorite letter?

B's. (Bees)

_____ /1

Why couldn't the statue cry?

It had a heart of stone!

_____ /1

JOKES TOTAL: _____ /4

Silly Scenarios

(Act it out!)

It's wintertime and the snow is soft and fluffy. Make your best snow angel! As soon as you're about to get up, you realize you're frozen to the ground. Keep trying!

/2

You are a bumble bee that loves flowers! Buzz around your friends as if they are flowers that are just blossoming!

/2

SILLY SCENARIOS TOTAL: _____ /4

TIME TO SCORE YOUR POINTS! ➔

ADD UP ALL YOUR POINTS FROM THE PREVIOUS ROUND. THE JESTER WITH THE MOST POINTS IS CROWNED THE ULTIMATE DON'T LAUGH CHALLENGE MASTER!

/8

JESTER 1

GRAND TOTAL

/8

JESTER 2

GRAND TOTAL

THE ULTIMATE
DON'T LAUGH CHALLENGE MASTER

Check out our

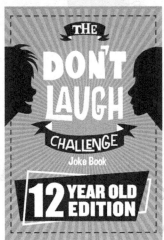

Visit us at
www.DontLaughChallenge.com
to check out our newest books!

other joke books!

If you have enjoyed our book, we would love for you to review us on Amazon!

Made in the USA
Monee, IL
03 November 2019

16133464R00046